THE BALLAD OF READING GAOL

THE BALLAD OF READING GAOL WAS FIRST PUBLISHED BY
LEONARD SMITHERS IN FEBRUARY 1898

THIS IS VOLUME TWO
IN THE CASTLE PRESS EDITION OF THE WORKS OF OSCAR WILDE

THE BALLAD
OF
READING GAOL

by Oscar Wilde

Illustrated by Arthur Wragg

LONDON
CASTLE PRESS

Other Works in this Series include:
by the same illustrator
LADY WINDERMERE'S FAN and AN IDEAL HUSBAND
illustrated by Michael Ayrton
THE PICTURE OF DORIAN GRAY

Made and Printed in Great Britain
for the
Castle Press
50 Old Brompton Road London SW7
by W S Cowell Ltd Ipswich
Designed by Vincent Stuart
First Impression October 1948

INTRODUCTION

by Arthur Wragg

'I AM not sure that I like it myself. But catastrophes in life bring about catastrophes in art.'

So said Wilde of this work, now generally regarded as his greatest achievement. Even Lord Alfred Douglas excepted it from his castigation of Wilde's writings.

It is his masterpiece because it was almost the only time he allowed himself to express a deep and genuine emotion which he regarded as æsthetically destructive to a work of art. Yet his Ballad gives more, demands more and *means* more than anything else he wrote. This achievement is due to the humiliation of a great but too facile mind; paradoxically, imprisonment released him from this facility and endowed him with qualities not to be found in the former Wilde.

In punishing him for a 'deviation' for which he could not be blamed, his world squeezed this final masterpiece from him not because it intended to, but because it could not destroy that which he had failed to destroy himself. His humiliation brought him painfully to see that what society could hate and avenge, God could accept and forgive.

Bitter and indignant as his Ballad justly is, it is yet an epic of forgiveness. Had it not been so it could not have transcended all that had gone before. It may be worthwhile, therefore, to look into the circumstances which provoked his cry of love and pain, heard more clearly now, perhaps, than fifty years ago.

Wilde was sent to Reading prison from Wandsworth where he had been ill. It was the second governor he encountered here, a Major Nelson, whom he grew to respect. It was due to him, to one or two warders and above all to his fellow-prisoners that he escaped the captive's final humiliation—

7

complete spiritual isolation. Though prisons all look alike from outside, the humans inside them differ as much as elsewhere and there are even a few warders who manage to survive the long years of discipline and still remain kindly men.

Warder Martin, of Reading Gaol, was one of these outstanding exceptions. The only things now known of Martin's existence are his kindness to Wilde and his 'weakness' for the giving of biscuits to child prisoners. It was the latter 'crime' which eventually caused his dismissal from the prison service shortly after Wilde's release.

Another warder collected Wilde's writings every morning for Major Nelson to read and returned them to the cell for Wilde to continue in the evenings. Possibly this gave the prisoner just enough stimulation to enable him to write and study, for he was not the type of man able to work in a vacuum. Yet his Ballad gives no hint of these things, as if the whole of his prison experience were bad. This is perhaps because he felt the intention of the prison machine as a whole to be bad and the individual rebels to exist only in spite of it—and there is no room for qualification in the compass of his verse. Our prisons today would still justify much of it, for on the whole they have improved very little if we compare them with our progress in more respectable directions.

The highest attainments of a certain kind of art are bound to be propagandic in character. The Ballad of Reading Gaol is propaganda bearing that mark of Truth which is the whole of art. It is threaded upon the most valuable of all human emotions—compassion, yet its rhythm is one of indignation and fury that man can inflict on man such terrible wrongs because they are backed by the law. We can do these things collectively (or have them done in our name) from which we would individually recoil. How many of us who believe in capital punishment would deliberately hang a man until he is dead?

Yet we pay someone else to do it—some stooge who will relieve us of our responsibility.

All who have worked in prisons, or who have been inside them at such times, would agree with every word of Wilde's poetic description of the effect upon other prisoners. This is Truth as it is seldom told, in a form which is both free from the fear of sentimentality and yet disciplined by the convention of the verse itself. I have been with prisoners whose ears were cocked for every sound and whose attention was distracted by a morbid interest in the cold inevitability of the coming day's event. I remember a young man, convinced his own end would be the same (and nearly had been), who waited for the ignoble death of his fellow-prisoner with the sweat of fear upon his own brow; for prison is a kind of captive twilight most theatrically suitable for the weaving of the inverted phantasy and the introspective terror so vividly conveyed in this poem.

* * * *

The Prison Commissioners were kind enough to allow me to visit Reading prison to see the background of the work. It is vastly changed since Wilde's time there and, I should imagine, considerably cheered by the work and personality of the present governor, Mr W. P. Harding. It had been closed for something like twenty-eight years and only recently reopened, so that the records have been removed and all tradition broken —for all prisons have traditions peculiarly their own.

It seemed to me much brighter and more congenial than, for instance, Wandsworth prison. It is certainly nothing like the prison Wilde knew. I was for a short time alone in his cell 'C.3.3.', which was the pseudonym under which he first published his Ballad. There was an old table-shelf in one corner, a fixture which must have dated from his time and upon which he may have planned some of these lines—the work was not completed, however, until after his release. The window was even smaller than most cell windows, and that part which opened to admit the air I judged to be about ten inches square. I sketched some of the details of his cell and of the galleries but I have not made use of them in these drawings because such material facts could only conflict with the nightmare quality of the verse itself. But in view of the poet's references to the gaol he knew, it may be interesting to note the following points gleaned from such records as I have been able to trace.

Whilst he was there, for instance, there were twenty-four juvenile prisoners all under the age of fifteen, including one girl of fourteen. The youngest prisoner was ten years old. Five of his fellow-prisoners were insane. The child-prisoner was a very common sight in our gaols until 1908. (A girl of not more than sixteen was hanged at Norwich prison in the same year as the events described in the Ballad—1896.)

The instruments of punishment are now largely forgotten; the 'crank' for instance, was a machine designed for hard labour, being a contraption which was merely difficult to turn. It produced nothing and served no purpose other than a kind of useless torture which the prisoner could enjoy in the privacy of his own cell. The crank and the Tread-'mill' were still being used well into this century.

Such things are not used in our prisons of 1948, but the two greatest evils of them all are still not abolished—flogging and hanging. The Ballad is the greatest indictment of judicial murder ever conceived and no one can read Wilde's passionate protest without experiencing some of his shame and indignation. There is nothing to add and no more to be said; the poem is to be judged by its purpose as well as its quality. Its purpose will not have been achieved until the final abolition of capital punishment—after that it will still remain one of the most moving works of art in the English language.

Polperro. 1948.

IN MEMORIAM
C. T. W.
SOMETIME TROOPER OF
THE ROYAL HORSE GUARDS
OBIIT H.M. PRISON
READING BERKSHIRE
JULY 7TH 1896

ONE

HE did not wear his scarlet coat,
   For blood and wine are red,
And blood and wine were on his hands
   When they found him with the dead,
The poor dead woman whom he loved,
   And murdered in her bed.

He walked amongst the Trial Men
   In a suit of shabby grey;
A cricket cap was on his head,
   And his step seemed light and gay;
But I never saw a man who looked
   So wistfully at the day.

I never saw a man who looked
   With such a wistful eye
Upon that little tent of blue
   Which prisoners call the sky,
And at every drifting cloud that went
   With sails of silver by.

I walked, with other souls in pain,
   Within another ring,
And was wondering if the man had done
   A great or little thing,
When a voice behind me whispered low,
   That fellow's got to swing.

Dear Christ! the very prison walls
  Suddenly seemed to reel,
And the sky above my head became
  Like a casque of scorching steel;
And, though I was a soul in pain,
  My pain I could not feel.

I only knew what hunted thought
  Quickened his step, and why
He looked upon the garish day
  With such a wistful eye;
The man had killed the thing he loved
  And so he had to die.

＊

YET each man kills the thing he loves,
  By each let this be heard,
Some do it with a bitter look,
  Some with a flattering word,
The coward does it with a kiss,
  The brave man with a sword!

Some kill their love when they are young,
  And some when they are old;
Some strangle with the hands of Lust,
  Some with the hands of Gold:
The kindest use a knife, because
  The dead so soon grow cold.

Some love too little, some too long,
   Some sell, and others buy;
Some do the deed with many tears,
   And some without a sigh:
For each man kills the thing he loves,
   Yet each man does not die.

He does not die a death of shame
   On a day of dark disgrace,
Nor have a noose about his neck,
   Nor a cloth upon his face,
Nor drop feet foremost through the floor
   Into an empty space.

He does not sit with silent men
   Who watch him night and day;
Who watch him when he tries to weep,
   And when he tries to pray;
Who watch him lest himself should rob
   The prison of its prey.

He does not wake at dawn to see
   Dread figures throng his room,
The shivering Chaplain robed in white,
   The Sheriff stern with gloom,
And the Governor all in shiny black,
   With the yellow face of Doom.

He does not rise in piteous haste
    To put on convict clothes,
While some coarse-mouthed Doctor gloats, and
    Each new and nerve-twitched pose,   [notes
Fingering a watch whose little ticks
    Are like horrible hammer-blows.

He does not know that sickening thirst
    That sands one's throat, before
The hangman with his gardener's gloves
    Slips through the padded door,
And binds one with three leathern thongs,
    That the throat may thirst no more.

He does not bend his head to hear
    The Burial Office read,
Nor, while the terror of his soul
    Tells him he is not dead,
Cross his own coffin, as he moves
    Into the hideous shed.

He does not stare upon the air
    Through a little roof of glass:
He does not pray with lips of clay
    For his agony to pass;
Nor feel upon his shuddering cheek
    The kiss of Caiaphas.

TWO

SIX weeks our guardsman walked the yard,
   In the suit of shabby grey:
His cricket cap was on his head,
  And his step seemed light and gay,
But I never saw a man who looked
  So wistfully at the day.

I never saw a man who looked
  With such a wistful eye
Upon that little tent of blue
  Which prisoners call the sky,
And at every wandering cloud that trailed
  Its ravelled fleeces by.

He did not wring his hands as do
  Those witless men who dare
To try to rear the changeling Hope
  In the cave of black Despair:
He only looked upon the sun,
  And drank the morning air.

He did not wring his hands nor weep,
  Nor did he peek or pine,
But he drank the air as though it held
  Some healthful anodyne;
With open mouth he drank the sun
  As though it had been wine!

And I and all the souls in pain,
    Who tramped the other ring,
Forgot if we ourselves had done
    A great or little thing,
And watched with gaze of dull amaze
    The man who had to swing.

And strange it was to see him pass
    With a step so light and gay,
And strange it was to see him look
    So wistfully at the day,
And strange it was to think that he
    Had such a debt to pay.

*

FOR oak and elm have pleasant leaves
    That in the spring-time shoot:
But grim to see is the gallows-tree,
    With its adder-bitten root,
And, green or dry, a man must die
    Before it bears its fruit!

The loftiest place is that seat of grace
　For which all worldlings try:
But who would stand in hempen band
　Upon a scaffold high,
And through a murderer's collar take
　His last look at the sky?

It is sweet to dance to violins
　When Love and Life are fair:
To dance to flutes, to dance to lutes
　Is delicate and rare:
But it is not sweet with nimble feet
　To dance upon the air!

So with curious eyes and sick surmise
　We watched him day by day,
And wondered if each one of us
　Would end the self-same way,
For none can tell to what red Hell
　His sightless soul may stray.

23

At last the dead man walked no more
  Amongst the Trial Men,
And I knew that he was standing up
  In the black dock's dreadful pen,
And that never would I see his face
  In God's sweet world again.

Like two doomed ships that pass in storm
  We had crossed each other's way:
But we made no sign, we said no word,
  We had no word to say;
For we did not meet in the holy night,
  But in the shameful day.

A prison wall was round us both,
  Two outcast men we were:
The world had thrust us from its heart,
  And God from out His care:
And the iron gin that waits for Sin
  Had caught us in its snare.

D

THREE

IN Debtors' Yard the stones are hard,
  And the dripping wall is high,
So it was there he took the air
  Beneath the leaden sky,
And by each side a Warder walked,
  For fear the man might die.

Or else he sat with those who watched
  His anguish night and day;
Who watched him when he rose to weep,
  And when he crouched to pray;
Who watched him lest himself should rob
  Their scaffold of its prey.

The Governor was strong upon
  The Regulations Act:
The Doctor said that Death was but
  A scientific fact:
And twice a day the Chaplain called,
  And left a little tract.

And twice a day he smoked his pipe,
  And drank his quart of beer:
His soul was resolute, and held
  No hiding-place for fear;
He often said that he was glad
  The hangman's hands were near.

But why he said so strange a thing
    No Warder dared to ask:
For he to whom a watcher's doom
    Is given as his task
Must set a lock upon his lips,
    And make his face a mask.

Or else he might be moved, and try
    To comfort or console:
And what should Human Pity do
    Pent up in Murderers' Hole?
What word of grace in such a place
    Could help a brother's soul?

With slouch and swing around the ring
    We trod the Fools' Parade!
We did not care: we knew we were
    The Devil's Own Brigade:
And shaven head and feet of lead
    Make a merry masquerade.

We tore the tarry rope to shreds
    With blunt and bleeding nails;
We rubbed the doors, and scrubbed the floors,
    And cleaned the shining rails:
And, rank by rank, we soaked the plank,
    And clattered with the pails.

We sewed the sacks, we broke the stones,
  We turned the dusty drill:
We banged the tins, and bawled the hymns,
  And sweated on the mill:
But in the heart of every man
  Terror was lying still.

So still it lay that every day
  Crawled like a weed-clogged wave:
And we forgot the bitter lot
  That waits for fool and knave,
Till once, as we tramped in from work,
  We passed an open grave.

With yawning mouth the yellow hole
  Gaped for a living thing;
The very mud cried out for blood
  To the thirsty asphalte ring:
And we knew that ere one dawn grew fair
  Some prisoner had to swing.

Right in we went, with soul intent
  On Death and Dread and Doom:
The hangman, with his little bag,
  Went shuffling through the gloom:
And each man trembled as he crept
  Into his numbered tomb.

*

THAT night the empty corridors
  Were full of forms of Fear,
And up and down the iron town
  Stole feet we could not hear,
And through the bars that hide the stars
  White faces seemed to peer.

He lay as one who lies and dreams
  In a pleasant meadow-land,
The watchers watched him as he slept,
  And could not understand
How one could sleep so sweet a sleep
  With a hangman close at hand.

But there is no sleep when men must weep
    Who never yet have wept:
So we—the fool, the fraud, the knave—
    That endless vigil kept,
And through each brain on hands of pain
    Another's terror crept.

Alas! it is a fearful thing
    To feel another's guilt!
For, right within, the sword of Sin
    Pierced to its poisoned hilt,
And as molten lead were the tears we shed
    For the blood we had not spilt.

The Warders with their shoes of felt
    Crept by each padlocked door,
And peeped and saw, with eyes of awe,
    Grey figures on the floor,
And wondered why men knelt to pray
    Who never prayed before.

All through the night we knelt and prayed,
    Mad mourners of a corse!
The troubled plumes of midnight were
    The plumes upon a hearse:
And bitter wine upon a sponge
    Was the savour of Remorse.

31

THE grey cock crew, the red cock crew,
    But never came the day:
And crooked shapes of Terror crouched
    In the corners where we lay:
And each evil sprite that walks by night
    Before us seemed to play.

They glided past, they glided fast,
    Like travellers through a mist:
They mocked the moon in a rigadoon
    Of delicate turn and twist,
And with formal pace and loathsome grace
    The phantoms kept their tryst.

With mop and mow, we saw them go,
    Slim shadows hand in hand:
About, about, in ghostly rout
    They trod a saraband:
And the damned grotesques made arabesques,
    Like the wind upon the sand!

With the pirouettes of marionettes,
    They tripped on pointed tread:
But with flutes of Fear they filled the ear,
    As their grisly masque they led,
And loud they sang, and long they sang,
    For they sang to wake the dead.

E

'*Oho!*' they cried, '*The world is wide,*
  But fettered limbs go lame!
And once, or twice, to throw the dice
  Is a gentlemanly game,
But he does not win who plays with Sin
  In the secret House of Shame.'

No things of air these antics were,
  That frolicked with such glee:
To men whose lives were held in gyves,
  And whose feet might not go free,
Ah! wounds of Christ! they were living things,
  Most terrible to see.

Around, around, they waltzed and wound;
　　Some wheeled in smirking pairs;
With the mincing step of a demirep
　　Some sidled up the stairs:
And with subtle sneer, and fawning leer,
　　Each helped us at our prayers.

The morning wind began to moan,
　　But still the night went on:
Through its giant loom the web of gloom
　　Crept till each thread was spun:
And, as we prayed, we grew afraid
　　Of the Justice of the Sun.

The moaning wind went wandering round
    The weeping prison-wall:
Till like a wheel of turning steel
    We felt the minutes crawl:
O moaning wind! what had we done
    To have such a seneschal?

At last I saw the shadowed bars,
    Like a lattice wrought in lead,
Move right across the whitewashed wall
    That faced my three-plank bed,
And I knew that somewhere in the world
    God's dreadful dawn was red.

At six o'clock we cleaned our cells,
    At seven all was still,
But the sough and swing of a mighty wing
    The prison seemed to fill,
For the Lord of Death with icy breath
    Had entered in to kill.

He did not pass in purple pomp,
    Nor ride a moon-white steed.
Three yards of cord and a sliding board
    Are all the gallows' need:
So with rope of shame the Herald came
    To do the secret deed.

We were as men who through a fen
    Of filthy darkness grope:
We did not dare to breathe a prayer,
    Or to give our anguish scope:
Something was dead in each of us,
    And what was dead was Hope.

For Man's grim Justice goes its way,
    And will not swerve aside:
It slays the weak, it slays the strong,
    It has a deadly stride:
With iron heel it slays the strong,
    The monstrous parricide!

We waited for the stroke of eight:
    Each tongue was thick with thirst:
For the stroke of eight is the stroke of Fate
    That makes a man accursed,
And Fate will use a running noose
    For the best man and the worst.

We had no other thing to do,
    Save to wait for the sign to come:
So, like things of stone in a valley lone,
    Quiet we sat and dumb:
But each man's heart beat thick and quick,
    Like a madman on a drum!

With sudden shock the prison-clock
   Smote on the shivering air,
And from all the gaol rose up a wail
   Of impotent despair,
Like the sound that frightened marshes hear
   From some leper in his lair.

And as one sees most fearful things
   In the crystal of a dream,
We saw the greasy hempen rope
   Hooked to the blackened beam,
And heard the prayer the hangman's snare
   Strangled into a scream.

And all the woe that moved him so
   That he gave that bitter cry,
And the wild regrets, and the bloody sweats,
   None knew so well as I:
For he who lives more lives than one
   More deaths than one must die.

F

FOUR

THERE is no chapel on the day
      On which they hang a man:
The Chaplain's heart is far too sick,
      Or his face is far too wan,
Or there is that written in his eyes
      Which none should look upon.

So they kept us close till nigh on noon,
      And then they rang the bell,
And the warders with their jingling keys
      Opened each listening cell,
And down the iron stair we tramped
      Each from his separate Hell.

Out into God's sweet air we went,
      But not in wonted way,
For this man's face was white with fear,
      And that man's face was grey,
And I never saw sad men who looked
      So wistfully at the day.

I never saw sad men who looked
      With such a wistful eye
Upon that little tent of blue
      We prisoners call the sky,
And at every careless cloud that passed
      In happy freedom by.

43

But there were those amongst us all
    Who walked with downcast head,
And knew that, had each got his due,
    They should have died instead:
He had but killed a thing that lived,
    Whilst they had killed the dead.

For he who sins a second time
    Wakes a dead soul to pain,
And draws it from its spotted shroud,
    And makes it bleed again,
And makes it bleed great gouts of blood
    And makes it bleed in vain!

*

LIKE ape or clown, in monstrous garb
    With crooked arrows starred,
Silently we went round and round
    The slippery asphalte yard;
Silently we went round and round,
    And no man spoke a word.

Silently we went round and round,
    And through each hollow mind
The Memory of dreadful things
    Rushed like a dreadful wind,
And Horror stalked before each man,
    And Terror crept behind.

THE Warders strutted up and down,
And kept their herd of brutes,
Their uniforms were spick and span,
And they wore their Sunday suits,
But we knew the work they had been at,
By the quicklime on their boots.

For where a grave had opened wide,
There was no grave at all:
Only a stretch of mud and sand
By the hideous prison-wall,
And a little heap of burning lime,
That the man should have his pall.

For he has a pall, this wretched man,
Such as few men can claim:
Deep down below a prison-yard,
Naked for greater shame,
He lies, with fetters on each foot,
Wrapt in a sheet of flame!

And all the while the burning lime
    Eats flesh and bone away;
It eats the brittle bone by night,
    And the soft flesh by day,
It eats the flesh and bone by turns,
    But it eats the heart alway.

*

FOR three long years they will not sow
    Or root or seedling there:
For three long years the unblessed spot
    Will sterile be and bare,
And look upon the wondering sky
    With unreproachful stare.

They think a murderer's heart would taint
   Each simple seed they sow.
It is not true! God's kindly earth
   Is kindlier than men know,
And the red rose would but blow more red,
   The white rose whiter blow.

Out of his mouth a red, red rose!
   Out of his heart a white!
For who can say by what strange way
   Christ brings His will to light,
Since the barren staff the pilgrim bore
   Bloomed in the great Pope's sight?

But neither milk-white rose nor red
  May bloom in prison-air;
The shard, the pebble, and the flint,
  Are what they give us there:
For flowers have been known to heal
  A common man's despair.

So never will wine-red rose or white,
  Petal by petal, fall
On that stretch of mud and sand that lies
  By the hideous prison-wall,
To tell the men who tramp the yard
  That God's Son died for all.

*

Yet though the hideous prison-wall
  Still hems him round and round,
And a spirit may not walk by night
  That is with fetters bound,
And a spirit may but weep that lies
  In such unholy ground.

He is at peace—this wretched man—
  At peace, or will be soon:
There is no thing to make him mad,
  Nor does Terror walk at noon,
For the lampless Earth in which he lies
  Has neither Sun nor Moon.

G

They hanged him as a beast is hanged:
  They did not even toll
A requiem that might have brought
  Rest to his startled soul,
But hurriedly they took him out,
  And hid him in a hole.

They stripped him of his canvas clothes,
  And gave him to the flies:
They mocked the swollen purple throat,
  And the stark and staring eyes:
And with laughter loud they heaped the shroud
  In which the convict lies.

The Chaplain would not kneel to pray
  By his dishonoured grave:
Nor mark it with that blessed Cross
  That Christ for sinners gave,
Because the man was one of those
  Whom Christ came down to save.

Yet all is well; he has but passed
  To Life's appointed bourne:
And alien tears will fill for him
  Pity's long-broken urn,
For his mourners will be outcast men,
  And outcasts always mourn.

FIVE

I KNOW not whether Laws be right,
   Or whether Laws be wrong;
All that we know who lie in gaol
   Is that the wall is strong;
And that each day is like a year,
   A year whose days are long.

But this I know, that every Law
   That men have made for Man,
Since first Man took his brother's life,
   And the sad world began,
But straws the wheat and saves the chaff
   With a most evil fan.

This too I know—and wise it were
   If each could know the same—
That every prison that men build
   Is built with bricks of shame,
And bound with bars lest Christ should see
   How men their brothers maim.

With bars they blur the gracious moon,
   And blind the goodly sun:
And they do well to hide their Hell,
   For in it things are done
That Son of God nor son of Man
   Ever should look upon!

*

THE vilest deeds, like poison weeds,
    Bloom well in prison-air;
It is only what is good in Man
    That wastes and withers there:
Pale Anguish keeps the heavy gate,
    And the Warder is Despair.

54

For they starve the little frightened child
   Till it weeps both night and day:
And they scourge the weak, and flog the fool,
   And gibe the old and grey,
And some grow mad, and all grow bad,
   And none a word may say.

Each narrow cell in which we dwell
  Is a foul and dark latrine,
And the fetid breath of living Death
  Chokes up each grated screen,
And all, but Lust, is turned to dust
  In Humanity's machine.

The brackish water that we drink
  Creeps with a loathsome slime,
And the bitter bread they weigh in scales
  Is full of chalk and lime,
And Sleep will not lie down, but walks
  Wild-eyed, and cries to Time.

*

But though lean Hunger and green Thirst
   Like asp with adder fight,
We have little care of prison fare,
   For what chills and kills outright
Is that every stone one lifts by day
   Becomes one's heart by night.

With midnight always in one's heart,
   And twilight in one's cell,
We turn the crank, or tear the rope,
   Each in his separate Hell,
And the silence is more awful far
   Than the sound of a brazen bell.

And never a human voice comes near
   To speak a gentle word:
And the eye that watches through the door
   Is pitiless and hard:
And by all forgot, we rot and rot,
   With soul and body marred.

And thus we rust Life's iron chain
   Degraded and alone:
And some men curse, and some men weep,
   And some men make no moan:
But God's eternal Laws are kind
   And break the heart of stone.

*

AND every human heart that breaks,
   In prison-cell or yard,
Is as that broken box that gave
   Its treasure to the Lord,
And filled the unclean leper's house
   With the scent of costliest nard.

Ah! happy they whose hearts can break
   And peace of pardon win!
How else may man make straight his plan
   And cleanse his soul from Sin?
How else but through a broken heart
   May Lord Christ enter in?

*

And he of the swollen purple throat,
  And the stark and staring eyes,
Waits for the holy hands that took
  The Thief to Paradise;
And a broken and a contrite heart
  The Lord will not despise.

The man in red who reads the Law
  Gave him three weeks of life,
Three little weeks in which to heal
  His soul of his soul's strife,
And cleanse from every blot of blood
  The hand that held the knife.

And with tears of blood he cleansed the hand,
  The hand that held the steel:
For only blood can wipe out blood,
  And only tears can heal:
And the crimson stain that was of Cain
  Became Christ's snow-white seal.

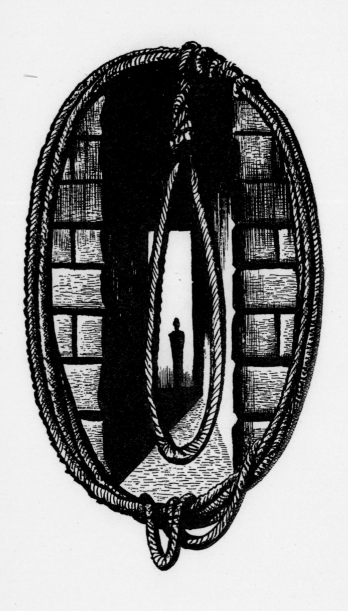

SIX

IN Reading gaol by Reading town
    There is a pit of shame,
And in it lies a wretched man
    Eaten by teeth of flame,
In a burning winding-sheet he lies,
    And his grave has got no name.

And there, till Christ call forth the dead,
    In silence let him lie:
No need to waste the foolish tear,
    Or heave the windy sigh:
The man had killed the thing he loved,
    And so he had to die.

And all men kill the thing they love,
    By all let this be heard,
Some do it with a bitter look,
    Some with a flattering word,
The coward does it with a kiss,
    The brave man with a sword!

McCullum
12.1.49.